Tideway

Jane Draycott is a UK-based poet with a particular interest in audio and collaborative work. Her publications include a recently reissued edition of *Christina the Astonishing* in collaboration with Lesley Saunders, (Two Rivers Press, 1998, reissued 2022), and *Storms Under the Skin* (2017), translations from the poems of artist-writer Henri Michaux, as well as five collections from Carcanet Press, including *The Occupant* (2016, Poetry Book Society Recommendation), *Over* (2009, T S Eliot Prize shortlist) and her prize-winning translation of the 14th-century dream-elegy *Pearl*. She teaches on postgraduate writing programmes at the universities of Oxford and Lancaster and is a Fellow of the Royal Society of Literature.

Also by Two Rivers Poets

David Attwooll, *The Sound Ladder* (2015)
Charles Baudelaire, *Paris Scenes* translated by Ian Brinton (2021)
William Bedford, *The Dancers of Colbek* (2020)
Kate Behrens, *Man with Bombe Alaska* (2016)
Kate Behrens, *Penumbra* (2019)
Kate Behrens, *Transitional Spaces* (2022)
Conor Carville, *English Martyrs* (2019)
David Cooke, *A Murmuration* (2015)
David Cooke, *Sicilian Elephants* (2021)
Tim Dooley, *Discoveries* (2022)
Jane Draycott & Lesley Saunders, *Christina the Astonishing*
    (re-issued 2022)
Claire Dyer, *Interference Effects* (2016)
Claire Dyer, *Yield* (2021)
John Froy, *Sandpaper & Seahorses* (2018)
James Harpur, *The Examined Life* (2021)
Maria Teresa Horta, *Point of Honour* translated by Lesley Saunders (2019)
Ian House, *Just a Moment* (2020)
Rosie Jackson & Graham Burchell, *Two Girls and a Beehive* (2020)
Gill Learner, *Chill Factor* (2016)
Gill Learner, *Change* (2021)
Sue Leigh, *Chosen Hill* (2018)
Sue Leigh, *Her Orchards* (2021)
Becci Louise, *Octopus Medicine* (2017)
Mairi MacInnes, *Amazing Memories of Childhood, etc.* (2016)
Steven Matthews, *On Magnetism* (2017)
Henri Michaux, *Storms under the Skin* translated by Jane Draycott (2017)
René Noyau, *Earth on Fire and other Poems* translated by Gérard Noyau
    with Peter Pegnall (2021)
James Peake, *Reaction Time of Glass* (2019)
James Peake, *The Star in the Branches* (2022)
Peter Robinson, *English Nettles* (re-issued 2022)
Peter Robinson & David Inshaw, *Bonjour Mr Inshaw* (2020)
Lesley Saunders, *Nominy-Dominy* (2018)
Lesley Saunders, *This Thing of Blood & Love* (2022)
Jack Thacker, *Handling* (2018)
Susan Utting, *Half the Human Race* (2017)
Jean Watkins, *Precarious Lives* (2018)

Tideway

Jane Draycott

Artwork by Peter Hay

First published in the UK in 2002 by Two Rivers Press
Second edition published 2022
7 Denmark Road, Reading RG1 5PA.
www.tworiverspress.com

© in texts and poems Jane Draycott 2002
© in paintings Peter Hay 2002
© in map of the Tideway Sally Castle 2022

The right of the poet to be identified as the author of this work has been asserted by her in accordance with the Copyright, Designs and Patents Act of 1988.

All rights reserved. No part of this publication may be reproduced, stored in or introduced into a retrieval system, or transmitted, in any form, or by any means (electronic, mechanical, photocopying, recording or otherwise) without the prior written permission of the publisher.

ISBN 987-1-915048-01-1

1 2 3 4 5 6 7 8 9

Two Rivers Press is represented in the UK by Inpress Ltd and distributed by Ingram Publisher Services UK.

Cover design by Nadja Guggi with a painting by Peter Hay
Text design by Nadja Guggi and typeset in Janson and Parisine

Printed and bound in Great Britain by Severn, Gloucester

Acknowledgements

2002

Very special thanks are due to the London watermen, divers, ship's pilots, police and other river workers who welcomed me with such hospitality, some of whose words feature in the pages of this book: Jane Andrews, Tom Burns, Sid Charles, Ken Dwan, Craig Edwards, Mark Edwards, Jimmy Gee, Chief Insp. Alan King, Chris Livett, Bob Lupton, Glen Luxton, Ted Maynard, Sgt Rod Mead, John Morton, Colin Murphy, Simon Murphy, Chas Newens, Peter Sargent, Luke Scott, Peter Skein, Peter Still, Tony Thomas and Mark Williams. Also Steve Colclough and Richard Oakleigh of the Environment Agency, Roger Mutton of the Port of London Authority, and David Pau and Kenny Martin working for Norwest/Costain.

Thanks are also due to Joy Ardy and Elizabeth Bell for their enthusiasm and wonderful supply of books, to Norman Price for his patience, to Sally Castle for her imagination and dedication and to Keiren Phelan for his unstinting interest in the idea since the beginning.

I am grateful to the editors of the following publications in which some of these poems first appeared: *The Bridport Prize Anthology 2000, Oxford Poets 2001 (Carcanet Press), Regatta Magazine* and *The Times Literary Supplement.* 'No 3 *from* Uses for the Thames' was originally commissioned by Southern Arts as a *Year of the Artist* postcard.

2022

Grateful thanks are due to the editors of *The Forward Book of Poetry 2003, 100 Prized Poems: Twenty-five Years of the Forward Books* and *The Guardian,* in which several of these poems appeared after *Tideway*'s first issue. Thanks are also due to Carcanet Press for their kind permission to reprint poems also collected in *The Night Tree* (Carcanet 2004), and to *Poems on the Underground* who featured 'No 3 *from* Uses for the Thames' as part of Transport for London's 2016 series 'London is Open', design by Tom Davidson.

My warm thanks go to Peter Robinson and Anne Nolan at Two Rivers Press for all their attentive enthusiasm for this re-issue, and most especially to Nadja Guggi for her beautiful book design and to Sally Castle for her fine new artwork on the inside covers.

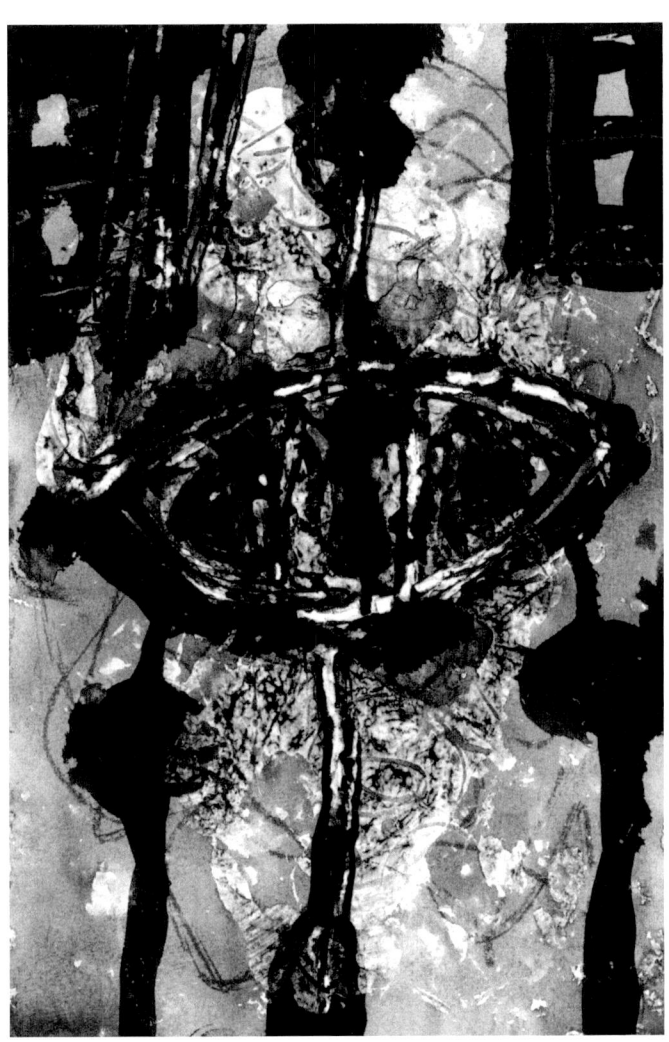

Contents

Preface to the first edition | ix
Introduction | x
A visual note by Peter Hay and Sally Castle | xiii

Tideway

Salvage | 1
Silvertown | 3
Public Records Office | 4
Cooling | 7

It's like a magnet working on the water | 8

Last Frost Fair | 10
Apprentice | 13
No. 3 *from* Uses for the Thames | 15
Surgeon | 16

Everyone who works on the river knows
who everyone else is | 18

Channel | 21
Here they come | 23
Shad Thames | 24
Tide | 25

All you'll see is reed rushes and cranes, and it's spooky | 26

St Mary Overie | 28
Waterman | 30
It begins | 31
City | 33

The water is their livelihood | 34

from Matchless | 36
   1. The Lost Girls | 36
   2. Out in the Twilight Zone | 37
   3. The Towers | 38
River | 41

Preface to the first edition

Last winter as part of a Southern Arts residency at Henley's River and Rowing Museum, I spent several weeks out on the tugs and barges of the London Thames collecting audio material for an exhibition about the working lives of the city's Company of Watermen. Travelling often from dawn to dusk, they were long days, waiting for the tides, watching the water and the skies.

This book brings the poems written during those months together with the paintings of Peter Hay and some of the words of the watermen themselves. Thrown to and fro over the radio, shouted across the water above the din of engine noise and wind, theirs is the image-rich language of a close-knit community with physically very wide horizons. It is a community in a state of transition: 25 years ago there were over 5000 watermen, then with containerisation came the wholesale transformation of the wharves and docklands. But there are still many hundreds of men, and a few women, who continue to work London's tideway night and day almost unnoticed and I owe many of them a sincere debt of thanks for their hospitality.

I would like the thank the Society of Authors and Southern Arts for their generous assistance during the preparation of the book, photographer Jaap Oepkes, together with Emily Leach and Alicia Gurney of the River and Rowing Museum for their support and companionship during the original residency, and Colin Middlemiss and Sara Kotch of the Company of Watermen and Lightermen for allowing us access to the archives at Watermen's Hall.

Jane Draycott, May 2002

Introduction

The origins of the first edition of *Tideway* were from the start a collaborative affair. Alongside the poems and Peter Hay's luminous watercolours, this book also contains the transcribed words of the London watermen whose accounts of their work on the water I recorded over a few dark winter weeks at the end of the year 2000. These highly skilled men – and one woman – gave of their time and patience as photographer Jaap Oepkes and I accompanied them at work on the Thames between Richmond and Erith. Jaap, a Dutch photographer with a deep understanding of rivers and waterways, was creating a new body of work for his memorable 2001 'Riverworks' exhibition at Henley's River & Rowing Museum, commissioned by London's Company of Watermen and Lightermen. His series of photographs, along with the recordings and a 2002 audio-montage *Salvage,* are now part of the archive at the Museum.

In the months that followed, the *Tideway* poems-in-progress which arrived then inspired artist and Two Rivers founder Peter Hay to paint the companion watercolour images which fill this collection with so much light. It was Pete who showed me, as we looked down into the city river together one murky afternoon, how light and dark moved inextricably in the stream together, and it is wonderful to see his paintings from that time given life on the page again in Nadja Guggi's wonderful new book design.

In the twenty years since *Tideway* was first published much has changed on London's working river. In the early years of the millennium, as traffic up and down river continued to slow following the redevelopment of docklands, wharves and warehouses, it was possible to stand on the embankment and see barely a working boat out, other than party boats, RIB speedboat rides and tourist-trip vessels. But today in 2022, large-scale infrastructure projects such as the new Thames Tunnel mean that the river has again become a route for freight in preference over slow-moving road transport, and according to the new Master at Watermen's Hall, boat operations more generally may be set to accelerate again. The river's network of passenger piers is expanding eastwards, ferries are back, and the increase in online shopping has generated new interest in the use of the river for the transportation of light freight and parcels.

In the same twenty years, Two Rivers Press has also significantly expanded its strong and flourishing reputation as an independent poetry publisher of bold design and illustration under the stewardship of poet-editors John Froy and, currently, Peter Robinson. The press's spirit of artistic collaboration lies very much at the heart of *Tideway's* original conception and it's a delight for that reason especially to see its new publication included as part of the Two Rivers Illustrated Classics series.

Jane Draycott, February 2022

A visual note

The paintings in this book are watercolours, with the exception of *River* (p. 40, acrylic and enamel) and *Titlepage* (p. vi, acrylic and ink), and are intended as companion pieces to Jane's wonderful words. They are imaginary topographies intuited from the light and shade of a sometimes sinister river. Techniques include the use of salt, clingfilm, masking fluid and wet-into-wet washes.

Peter Hay, 2002

Involvement with this reprint of *Tideway* brought back memories of working on the first edition. On a research trip with Jane and Peter to London, we walked alongside the river to the Watermen's Hall to see records written in copperplate – a style of writing I learnt as a child by copying lines of looping script with a dip pen. This time-honoured skill was used again for the Tideway map artwork inside the covers of this book.

The names and landmarks are not precisely positioned but represent the history of the Tideway area and the use of these names in a modern context loaded with memories of the past.

Sally Castle, 2022

Salvage

At his heels all the bigger rooms –
day, night, air – have closed their doors
as blindfold he enters the attic of the water.

Like particles of sleep mud raises itself
to his mask, and with his mind's eye
he fingers the darkness for signs of her.

This is the underworld of the deliberately lost,
the unforeseen consequence, MOT failure or weapon,
the barges for whom the river has all got too much.

Draped in silt, the debris delivers itself
to his fingertips, soft as the edges of thought,
as a handbrake left off, as the key to a previous door.

Far off he hears the approaching engine
of her name, a deep chest knocking. In his hand
the blue flame flowers and he begins to cut.

Slowly he surfaces and in the empty air
of the house the river runs off his face like a song.

Silvertown

Where the street was a valley
and each ship in its turn
a colossus or cliff at the mouth

out of which you might dream
you could slip like a sea-going question
or Lemuel Gulliver longing for more.

But the sun was our gold, thrown down
for the children to catch as they could
between shadows for hopscotch

and scars cast by derricks and spars,
and at full moon the alleys were paved
with something like silver

then the lines became threads
just powerful enough to tie a man down
and the ship seemed to shrink

become part of the sky
with its far away stars to navigate by
and tell us just where we were now –
the hammer, the pan, the plough.

Public Records Office

'If you would see something quite dreadful, go to the
enormous palace in the Strand, called Somerset House…
What can men do in such a catacomb?'
—Taine, *Notes sur Angleterre*

Ink comes in on the tide and with the watermen
and moths cuts up the stairs. Witnesses crowd
the courtyard in pairs, details are lost in the rain.

Behind the dead windows darkness is swallowing
the *Aula lucis*, the hall of light, like a sword:
year by year, marriage by marriage, a steady hand.

Last night, another murder in the watergardens.
Torches doused, the facts sit in pools on the flags
and that blind old allegory the Thames refuses to speak.

No mention here of those unaccountably let off
the hook, of the dates they were not with their friends
in the runaway hackneys, the train wrecks

or warships which broke like a biscuit, cordite
gangfiring back like a family tree through torpedo room,
ocean, the North Sea, past sandbanks and home.

In the river, the house and its offices hang like a ship
smeared with soot and the memory of flame underwater.

Cooling

for Keiren

In from the Scandinavias
the vast blank bandages haul
up the deep cut of the tideway

tomorrow's sagas emerging
through numberless mornings
of mist, page after page.

Beneath the city's amber chains
a brotherhood of barges waits
like hot metal cooling, destination

not yet known, swings on the hinge
of slack water, opening, closing,
prepares to face the other way.

Elsewhere a man makes ready
to take his small boat home, out
across the musculature of mud.

Like his father before him
he's watching for the whaleback
of the tide to take him down

toward Shivering Sand, the sea ahead
a pile of stories waiting to be read.

It's like a magnet working on the water

You can't see anything. Everything's done by touch. When you're cutting, you can just see the little blue flame on the end of the rod. That's all. You've got all sorts of things going on down there.

> Anybody that says they're not scared
> when they're in the water is a liar.

Coming down below Star and Garter hill of a summer's evening, the valley is very wide. Your horizons are further away.

> It's neither salt water and it's neither fresh water. It's brackish. With 5 or 6 knot tides it's always dangerous – if you go in you make your own chances. It's got so many turns and so many bridges that you've got to know what you're a doing of or you'll wind up in trouble.

The sound you can't ever forget is the wash and rush of the tide, the way the tide falls across the river.

> It's like a magnet, the working on the water.
> I have worked ashore – in a fur factory once –
> but I only stuck that for two hours.
> Couldn't stand being indoors.

We haven't got any radar in these small boats. Sometimes in the fog you do it by smell – you can smell Tate & Lyle's, like rum. You can smell the bone factory, the rubbish barges, the sewage works. You used to be able to smell the tea, the spice wharves, the wheat. You can smell your way up and down the river really.

> When I first come afloat all this was full up with ships
> and barges, all the way up. You could almost walk across
> on them. Now there's hardly anything. Wherever you look they're
> building houses – all working wharves at one time.

I think there's more watermen driving taxis than afloat now,
but then that's what they were originally, taking passengers
across to the theatres and the brothels.

> See that there, that's Convoy's, the last wharf to close.
> They used to get reels of newsprint come up there for the
> Daily Mirror group. That's a lovely berth. It all goes by
> road from the Medway now.

In those days watermen worked hard. They would physically
have to row with the tide, against the tide in rail, hail, wind, snow
or storm, dark or daylight. They had to row to survive.

> The air and the spray used to turn the bells and the whistles
> and the handrails green in a matter of hours. Brasswork taught
> me and other boys to appreciate a vessel.

They know everything there is to know – the set of the tides,
the history, the wharves, the reaches, the signals. They know
everything. They're totally different characters to anyone you've
ever met.

Last Frost Fair

'I should like to know what there is beneath us'
—Lieut. H. R. Bowers, Antarctica 1912

Lower Hope Point. Brought away by the pull
of the moon, glass slides towards the east.
At Blackfriars the ice remains solid and silent
like something completed or maybe about to begin.

In the opium dawn see how the air falls through
to the other side of nothing and survives.
Is it not amazing how the man continues to write?
Remarkably fine here on this limitless snow plain.

He dreams they are roasting a sheep, that someone
has driven a coach and four down from Queenhithe
and right through the tent. We have sandpapered
the runners, this has made a tremendous difference.

At the plying places wherrymen clear the way
for walking on water and the talk is all of the plumber
who ventured to cross with the lead in his hands.
The lord only knows how deep these chasms go.

Clairvoyants gaze at the accidents formed in the frost
while printers' boys carve their names in the monument
of the ice, sell papers to punters to prove they were there
at the last winter fair on this white village green

with its swingboats and puppet-shows, streamers
and flags like an army waved off to a war.
This afternoon 5.2 miles. The writing on the water.
The ash-strewn paths. Your name here.

Apprentice

'Come with me, though the wave is wild'
—Shelley, 'To William Shelley'

His hair is a flag and openly like fields
   he faces the coming water. His mind fills
with floating pieces of the jigsaw – bridges
   reaches, currents, wharves. Night signals. Knowledge.

His father will tell him what to remember.
   Not the hard hand of the wind in December
but the days of colliers loaded with labour,
   not the cave or gap at the foot of the ladder

but nights on the jetty watching for ships from Greece.
   The river doesn't scare him with its deepset looks,
its endlessly provisional position.
   He stands on the steel, a still point round which things

burn or float to sea. Canary Wharf is crowned
   in polar cloud. Limehouse is Table Mountain.
The freemen, passing, test him on the radio
   to check the things he does not know – how you

can leave and not come back again, how certain
   things are snatched away and certain things remain.

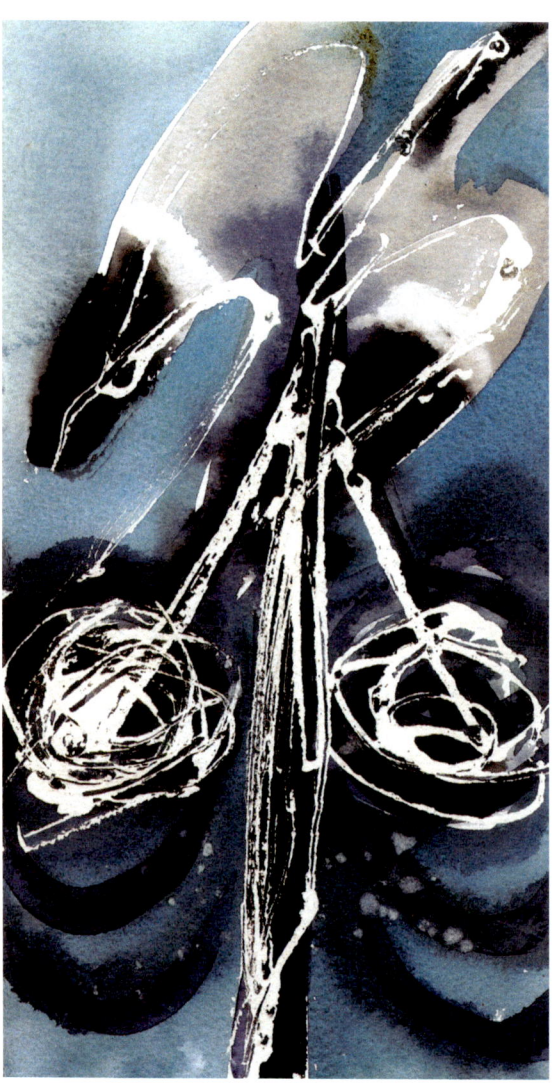

No. 3 *from* Uses for the Thames

'"Feather!" cried the Sheep ...'
—Lewis Carroll, *Through the Looking-Glass*

The test was to dip
the needles into the dark
of the swallowing mirror

and by pulling to row
the weight of your own small self
through the silvery jam of its surface

trailing behind in your passing
your very own tale, knitted
extempore from light

and then to lift them,
feathered, ready for flight.

Surgeon

He swims just before dawn, breasting the river
like a hill, parting it with his arms like a dancer
or priest. Ahead, a flat line of light divides
the two dark halves of the world from each other.

The air leans up to his face and with his ears only
he senses the dark landscape of the water,
its prostrate fields and struggling hedges,
its low-lying ridges and flooded verges.

Below the surface pearls of half-light, silver
with oxygen, cling like prayer beads to his fingers.
He is thinking about the anatomy of the heart,
the forks in the road, the red caves and narrow lanes

and on the horizon the possibility of a cathedral,
the sun rising like a corpuscle, winter wheat.

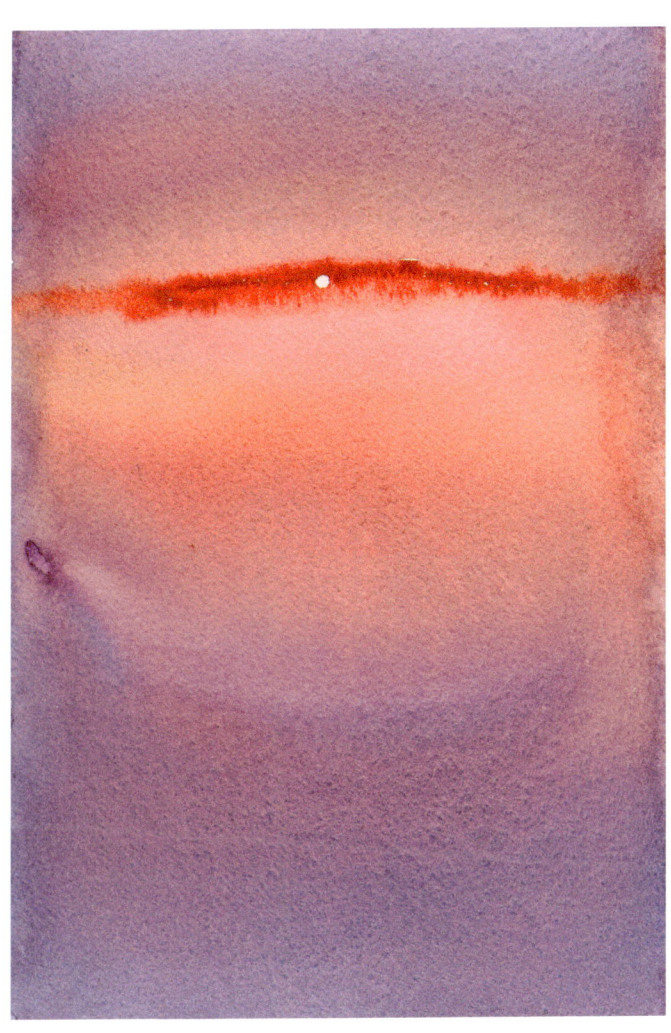

Everyone who works on the river knows who everyone else is

You name it, it's all in here. Cars, motorbikes, scaffolding,
trolleys, donkeys. Horses which got drowned in the fields, dogs
drowned on the foreshore. They float down from Richmond then
people complain about the thing lying in the river, and we have
to go and get it out. Mind you, a stolen Porsche ain't much
use to anyone when it's covered in silt.

                         The best noise is the hum of the engine
                            because it means you've got work.

Ships don't behave properly in the wind. The storm of 1987
we were working aboard the sugar ship, the wind got hold of me,
swept me right along the deck and I fetched up at the front there.
Then it went very still and gusted again and it was very hot,
about 3 in the morning. And it was full of sand. It had come up
from the Sahara, dust all over the ships, dust from the Sahara.

               The men all used to go out with one anothers' wives.

The moon makes a lot of difference, a very thin moon
and it can be very, very dark.

I know all the words necessary in about 6 languages. I can tell them
    to slack away, I can tell them to heave up, and I can do it in Greek,
              Filipino, Indian, Russian, Scandinavian, Dutch, German.
                    Because I've heard it so often. It sounds like
                         I understand their language
                and they have a bit of confidence in me then.

We were strong trade unionists.

    Barges banging, ships blowing, tugs blowing, everyone having a good swear and a laugh. Good sounds. Dockology they call it. That's our own language.

Everyone who works on the river knows who everyone else is. You can't have any secrets: I can tell something to someone down here at seven in the morning and hear the same story ten times bigger upriver at the end of the day.

    It's like a great elongated village 40 miles long. You see people every day, you don't know their names but you always say hi to them as they go past. It is a close community, yes.

If you told a docker they was going to turn these wharves into luxury apartments he'd say, 'Well they'd better clear the rats out of these warehouses first'.

    I'll never forget the first time I towed down to Shellhaven of an evening – all the lights and flares and gas being burned off. Even if you took a photo it wouldn't be the same.

On certain days you can smell the spices fallen through the floorboards. They say it's an added bonus for the residents. They do like that.

Channel

'the water comes and goes over itself – nine miles down
then eight and a half back up again'

>the water is a puzzle

>which takes a lot

>of thought

>to bring in goods

>take away goods

>and take water for cooling

>they took turns

>rather like taxi drivers

>put it into boats and took it

>to a place called the Black Deep

>I've seen that boat

>going past

>a few times

a reek<

of salt<

and mud<

seaweed<

and nameless jetsam<

lovely jubbly<

it's not so much now<

because they've killed it<

in smears of darkness<

a chaplet of lights<

growing less<

decipherable<

every<
moment<

Acknowledgments: Patrick Leigh Fermor *A Time of Gifts*

Here they come

'What odd things people throw away from ships'
—E. Arnot Robinson, *Thames Portrait*

Here they come, each leading the other forward
down the green lit corridor to the one-way ward

the battered sun-hat and the half a pierrot's costume
pale arms flailing for the memory of how to swim

the stricken deck-chair and the books, split-hinged
and lost, all bearings that they ever had on anything

the abandoned lengths of prostrate Baltic timber,
the waving shirt so like a white flag at a window.

Like articles thrown for good to the back of the mind
they circle each other on the bedlam of the ebbing tide

and as they float each views both riverbed and sky.
It is a meditation, like torn sails after a long journey.

Shad Thames

She has come to the river to trade
on her future, cash in on a single existence
here in the empty stomach of the warehouse.

At night she lies with the darkening map
of her hair on the pillow and listens to the rain
discharging its deep dyes on to the dockside.

On the skin of the water, heaving and passing,
the men. In her room the timber unshackles
the spices, spores flaring, a rumour of riot.

Later she watches the oil till it smokes
then gently lowers the powders and seeds.
As they move, change colour, transform.

She imagines herself turning slowly,
offering the complex history of her past,
the code of her hair, the other foreign place

inside her, and him putting her to his mouth,
as if you could eat it, lie down on a couch
and remember – shadows, nothing distinct.

Tide

'The Earl of Essex's locks of hair are on loan
to the Tower of London and will be back
on display in April.'
—The National Trust, Ham House

Recalled through the looking-glass plane
to the other side of the water, you wake
on an anti-material pillow of stone

to a polar bear dancing in chains,
the unbearable ravens, her majesty's
smack on the face again and again.

No hope that by hanging around
near the countrified jetties and orangeries
you'd escape the black hole of the city

the groans of the moat at the fall of the tide
the unobserved blows to the nape of the neck,
the hour when one becomes minus one.

You've been told you'll be back in the spring.
But try as you might you cannot make out
exactly the spot where the whole thing reverses,

the river, the objects, the life behind glass.

All you'll see is reed rushes and cranes, and it's spooky

We're called the buoy jumpers, lashing the ropes for the big ships. In an open boat like this it can be risky. We've had boats squashed before. I've had an anchor dropped on me once, the boat sank and we had to swim for it. You have to be a little bit lively.

> It's just like having buckets of water thrown over you sometimes, with the wind against the tide. But it's all I've ever wanted to do since I was a little boy with my dad.

It's more than a job. You can go to work at 3 in the morning and you'll be sitting on the jetty on a warm night waiting for a ship, and you've got time to think, take everything in.

> I've been on boats on this river all my life. There's people out there remember me since before I was born – they remember my mum pregnant with me on the boat with my dad.

When you're down in the cabin of a tug below the water, you hear the propellers of any shipping running past, it's like an echo, and you can tell from the echo was [what?] sort of ship it is.

> We've had young YTS lads who come and think, that looks good. It always does look good in the summer. It's when it comes to the winter it doesn't look so good. When it's snowing.

The river is being denied to people. The slipways are being closed. I remember the smell of burning tar, of the hot rivets, the smell of oakum. That's all finished up here.

When I was a little boy there was no green algae along the foreshore or on the walls, it was bleached white by the poisonous water on the Putney embankment. Today there's plants growing out of every crevice.

> Working on the party boats is just about all there is left so you have to take it. In the summer I'm home late after clearing up the boat, and I have to get going again at 4am. I'd much rather be outdoors on a tug, where you'd be utilising your licences, working with ropes, in the wheelbox handling the barges, not cleaning.

You're piloting a ship in Barking Creek at two o'clock in the morning in the pitch black and you can't see where you're going. All you'll see is reed rushes and cranes, and it's spooky. But we're the ones know how to do it.

> They told me I wouldn't stick it out, that when I got a boyfriend I'd give up. But I came back to work when my little girl was 3 and half months old, just because I was determined to finish it. And now I've got my licences and nobody can ever take that away.

St Mary Overie*

To Mary over the ferry
a single ticket taken,
to press the features into the pale
beyond the body of this water.

To Slut Lane let him be carried
a pilgrim by the boatman,
led by the spill of the vapour trail
and the milky way's stigmata.

To Mary over the ferry
a single ticket taken:
to Veronica her sky print veil,
to the water woman a daughter.

---

* The parish church of St Saviour and St Mary Overie (later Southwark Cathedral), located in an area traditionally best known for its brothels

Waterman

'It's all finished. There's only one boat out, and that's us.'

In his eyes it is all winter,
the water stopped like a glacier,
the men's skin grey, hearts frozen
like compass needles at the moment of the crime,
the boat locked in its repeating chapter
from the old boat story, and at the edge
like a series of tasks, the riverbank
struggling to make its way upstream.

It begins

'The lightermen used to buy their pipes pre-packed, then throw them overboard. Not so many of us smoke now.'

It begins as with razors or lighters
its sharpness or fire akin to a ship
that is passing, a fragment or sample
of something much bigger and further away
such as fathomless caverns of silver,
whole acres of indigo, saffron or hemp
or hillside on hillside of spices or tea
laid out like a rug to lie down on and sleep.
By capping the bowl like the door
to a furnace some made it last longer,
run cooler for breathing in deeper
its skyfuls of clouds, so that burdens
grown lighter could rise in the water
like palaces turning to smoke,
but a pipe once alight is a dream
which is now or is never and ends
like a pile of disposable bones
washed up on the foreshore
where in the same place the body
of a river ran just hours before.

City

for MH

The design of lower windows
suggests that their sun shone upwards
towards the surface of the water

their slipways of light emerging
from cellars of half-finished sentences
and dreams of wealthy philanthropists.

Towards the estuary it is possible to make out
the remains of several fishermen's huts
thrown up no doubt in the cataclysm

along with fragments of netting and sky,
and in one place the cast of the unfinished space
between a woman's hands is clearly visible.

The water is their livelihood

It looks different every day. If you wanted to paint that sky
and that river there, people would say no, you couldn't have
a sky and a river looking like that.

>The wind just took him and blew him over the side. They was
giving Force 8 or 9 and it was ebb tide, really humping down.
We had to leave the wheel to try to chuck a rope down to him.
After a lot of ducking and diving we eventually managed to
fish him out – he's one lucky man.

The water will carry you around but it won't let you surface.
You don't know where it's going to take you or what it's going
to do. You've only got a few seconds.

>You've got to forgo any sort of social life. Last week we had
three 4 a.m. orders, finishing about 9 at night. You're always waiting
for the tides – it's all governed by the moon.

They used to come back from South Africa then have five weeks
in London. Now it's five or six hours and they're away again.
One tide and they're gone.

>Once it gave work to thousands of men, but it's just
memories really.

There's been a lot of people jumping recently. There's no rhyme
nor reason.

>River life is traditional life, there's no two ways about it.
It's just something about the river, something that hangs on,
and it'll hang on for ever.

The smell of the diesel is always with you – on your clothes,
on your skin.

>What you get after all your years as apprentice
is your Freedom.

First thing you do is look at what the tide's doing, then you look up
for a friendly boat. If you see one you give him a wave. If not, you'll
catch him again tomorrow.

>Early morning, just as the dark is lifting off the water,
out in a tug with a full head of steam to a nice clear morning,
that's my picture.

If something goes wrong at night, people can't see. If someone
falls in and you miss them you may never get them back again.

from Matchless

1. The Lost Girls

Lost to their fathers flawless
and small they slip, Margery
Rita and Pearl, into sleep
one August embankment
all gates locked, laughing, leaving.

Across the water distant
and dream-led wander the men
cliff-faced by crystal and quartz,
splendid as winter, forested,
following the girls with their eyes.

In their dreams they are diving
for faces pale as perfection
searching the stream-beds and streets,
the forests of flyovers,
deeper and deeper they dive.

Each imagines on waking
he's found her, the woman
he knows is only a child
set like a lamp by a river,
lifting the phone to ring home.

2. Out in the Twilight Zone

Blown like cloud down the boardwalks
and reaches, loose limbed, dateless,
spun in the limitless wind –
all roads open eight till late,
this is the time of their lives.

Evening comes on in houseboats
and hotels, the upside-down
world reappears where less luck
is more luck, darkness is light
and last on the list might be first.

Out all night, oil in the wash
of police boats, the river's
their guide to life beyond home –
cold, fast, a wide enough wound
to drag them any distance.

At last sleep falls on the steps
of offices in whose files
if they looked they'd only find
themselves innocent. Streets off
the men stop, straining to hear.

3. The Towers

Morning matchless hits the fire
escapes, contact prints the day
she will wake to: the creeping
sense that someone has taken
her photograph while she slept.

Then rain and helicopters
hung like body bags from blades
cross the city, radio down
the news from the other side
it looks like hell down there.

At last the towers shift, lift
their shadows to leave less night
in kitchens and missions. Charged
with one half-life the voices
of girls gather like water.

On cloudless paper they write :
*these shadows, this waterside
dreaming's a region we can't
be brought home from*, their words
torn sidelong under the bridge.

River

Call it night, of the sort
with no edges or face
or reflection, a fault-line
of sleeplessness stirring
in tunnels and porches of churches,
a vessel for persons
gone missing or ready to go.

Call it fire, of the kind
which refuses to stop after curfew
but rips through the heart of the city
from neckline to navel
then spreads through the streets
like the lines of a play
that everyone knows ends in death.

Call it plague, of the type
with no signposts, a secret invasion
down blackened-out streets infected
with fear, a fast-flowing rumour,
a shadow which lives
in the bloodstream, the night-time
which runs through the day.

Two Rivers Press has been publishing in and about Reading
since 1994. Founded by the artist Peter Hay (1951–2003),
the press continues to delight readers, local and further afield,
with its varied list of individually designed,
thought-provoking books.

Barking Creek · *Barrier* · *Gallions Reach* · *Pier* · *Royal Victoria Dock* · *East India Dock* · *Royal Albert Dock* · *King George V Dock* · *Silvertown* · *Manhattan Wharf* · *Woolwich Reach* · *Tate & Lyle Wharf* · *Bellmouth Point* · **Thames Flood Barrier** · **Mud** · **Woolwich Ferry** · **Woolwich Dockyard** · *Blackcraft* · *Piper's Wharf* · *Lovell's Wharf* · *Mudlarks*